50 Easy Mexican Salsa and Dip Recipes for Home

By: Kelly Johnson

Table of Contents

- Classic Pico de Gallo
- Mango Salsa
- Roasted Tomato Salsa
- Pineapple Salsa
- Corn and Black Bean Salsa
- Avocado Salsa
- Tomatillo Salsa Verde
- Cilantro Lime Salsa
- Chipotle Tomato Salsa
- Watermelon Mint Salsa
- Grilled Peach Salsa
- Roasted Red Pepper Salsa
- Three-Bean Dip
- Guacamole
- Queso Blanco Dip
- Spinach and Artichoke Dip
- Jalapeño Popper Dip
- Corn and Jalapeño Dip
- Mango Avocado Salsa
- Roasted Garlic Salsa
- Roasted Corn Salsa
- Black Bean and Corn Dip
- Tomatillo Avocado Salsa
- Roasted Poblano Salsa
- Cucumber Salsa
- Mexican Street Corn Dip
- Pineapple Mango Guacamole
- Habanero Peach Salsa
- Fajita Queso Dip
- Creamy Jalapeño Dip
- Green Olive and Jalapeño Salsa
- Charred Tomato and Onion Salsa
- Tequila Lime Salsa
- Smoky Chipotle Guacamole
- Avocado Lime Crema

- Creamy Black Bean Dip
- Roasted Hatch Chile Salsa
- Roasted Serrano Salsa
- Roasted Pineapple Habanero Salsa
- Mango Habanero Guacamole
- Cilantro Lime Crema
- Black-Eyed Pea Salsa
- Chipotle Mango Salsa
- Tomatillo Guacamole
- Spicy Mango Pineapple Salsa
- Creamy Avocado Lime Salsa
- Roasted Garlic Guacamole
- Black Bean and Mango Salsa
- Smoky Tomatillo Salsa
- Roasted Jalapeño Guacamole

Classic Pico de Gallo

Ingredients:

- 4 medium tomatoes, diced
- 1 small red onion, finely chopped
- 1/2 cup fresh cilantro, chopped
- 1-2 jalapeño peppers, seeded and finely chopped (adjust to taste)
- 3 cloves garlic, minced
- Juice of 2 limes
- Salt and pepper to taste

Instructions:

In a large bowl, combine the diced tomatoes, chopped red onion, cilantro, jalapeño peppers, and minced garlic.
Squeeze the juice of 2 limes over the mixture.
Gently toss all the ingredients together until well combined.
Season the Pico de Gallo with salt and pepper to taste. Start with a pinch of salt and adjust according to your preference.
Refrigerate the Pico de Gallo for at least 30 minutes before serving to allow the flavors to meld.
Before serving, give the Pico de Gallo a final gentle stir.
Serve the Classic Pico de Gallo with tortilla chips, tacos, grilled meats, or your favorite Mexican dishes.

Enjoy this fresh and vibrant Pico de Gallo as a delicious topping or dip!

Mango Salsa

Ingredients:

- 2 ripe mangoes, peeled, pitted, and diced
- 1/2 red onion, finely chopped
- 1 red bell pepper, diced
- 1 jalapeño pepper, seeded and finely chopped
- 1/4 cup fresh cilantro, chopped
- Juice of 2 limes
- Salt and pepper to taste

Instructions:

In a mixing bowl, combine the diced mangoes, red onion, red bell pepper, jalapeño pepper, and cilantro.

Squeeze the juice of 2 limes over the mixture. Adjust the amount of lime juice based on your taste preferences.

Gently toss the ingredients together until well combined.

Season the mango salsa with salt and pepper to taste. Start with a small amount and adjust as needed.

Allow the salsa to chill in the refrigerator for at least 15-30 minutes before serving to enhance the flavors.

Before serving, give the mango salsa a final stir and adjust the seasoning if necessary.

Serve the Mango Salsa as a refreshing topping for grilled chicken, fish, tacos, or enjoy it with tortilla chips.

This Mango Salsa is a delightful combination of sweetness, tanginess, and a hint of heat. Enjoy!

Roasted Tomato Salsa

Ingredients:

- 6 medium-sized tomatoes, halved
- 1 onion, peeled and quartered
- 3 cloves garlic, peeled
- 2 jalapeño peppers, halved and seeds removed (adjust for spice preference)
- 1 tablespoon olive oil
- Salt and pepper to taste
- 1/4 cup fresh cilantro, chopped
- Juice of 1 lime

Instructions:

Preheat your oven to 400°F (200°C).

Place the halved tomatoes, quartered onion, garlic cloves, and halved jalapeño peppers on a baking sheet.

Drizzle the vegetables with olive oil and season with salt and pepper. Toss to coat evenly.

Roast the vegetables in the preheated oven for about 20-25 minutes or until the edges of the tomatoes and peppers are slightly charred.

Remove the baking sheet from the oven and let the roasted vegetables cool for a few minutes.

Transfer the roasted vegetables to a food processor or blender. Add chopped cilantro and lime juice.

Pulse the mixture until you achieve your desired salsa consistency. If you prefer a chunkier salsa, pulse fewer times.

Taste the salsa and adjust the seasoning with additional salt, pepper, or lime juice as needed.

Allow the Roasted Tomato Salsa to cool to room temperature, and then refrigerate for at least 30 minutes before serving to allow the flavors to meld.

Serve the salsa with tortilla chips, tacos, grilled meats, or your favorite Mexican dishes.

Enjoy the rich, smoky flavor of this Roasted Tomato Salsa!

Pineapple Salsa

Ingredients:

- 1 cup fresh pineapple, finely diced
- 1/2 red onion, finely chopped
- 1 red bell pepper, diced
- 1 jalapeño pepper, seeded and finely chopped
- 1/4 cup fresh cilantro, chopped
- Juice of 1 lime
- Salt and pepper to taste

Instructions:

In a bowl, combine the diced pineapple, chopped red onion, diced red bell pepper, chopped jalapeño, and cilantro.

Squeeze the juice of 1 lime over the mixture. Adjust the lime juice to your taste. Gently toss the ingredients together until well combined.

Season the pineapple salsa with salt and pepper to taste. Start with a small amount and adjust as needed.

Allow the salsa to sit in the refrigerator for at least 15-30 minutes before serving to let the flavors meld.

Before serving, give the pineapple salsa a final stir and adjust the seasoning if necessary.

Serve this Pineapple Salsa as a refreshing topping for grilled chicken, fish, shrimp, or as a side for tacos. It's also perfect with tortilla chips!

Enjoy the tropical sweetness and tanginess of this Pineapple Salsa!

Corn and Black Bean Salsa

Ingredients:

- 1 can (15 oz) black beans, drained and rinsed
- 1 cup corn kernels (fresh or frozen, thawed)
- 1 red bell pepper, finely diced
- 1/2 red onion, finely chopped
- 1 jalapeño pepper, seeded and finely chopped
- 1/4 cup fresh cilantro, chopped
- Juice of 2 limes
- 2 tablespoons olive oil
- 1 teaspoon ground cumin
- Salt and pepper to taste

Instructions:

In a large bowl, combine the black beans, corn kernels, diced red bell pepper, chopped red onion, chopped jalapeño, and chopped cilantro.

In a small bowl, whisk together the lime juice, olive oil, ground cumin, salt, and pepper.

Pour the dressing over the salsa ingredients.

Gently toss everything together until the salsa is well combined and coated in the dressing.

Taste the salsa and adjust the seasoning if needed, adding more salt, pepper, or lime juice according to your preferences.

Refrigerate the Corn and Black Bean Salsa for at least 30 minutes before serving to allow the flavors to meld.

Before serving, give the salsa a final stir and garnish with additional cilantro if desired.

Serve the salsa with tortilla chips, alongside grilled chicken or fish, or as a topping for tacos.

Enjoy the hearty and flavorful combination of corn and black beans in this delicious salsa!

Avocado Salsa

Ingredients:

- 2 ripe avocados, diced
- 1 medium tomato, diced
- 1/4 cup red onion, finely chopped
- 1 jalapeño pepper, seeded and finely chopped
- 1/4 cup fresh cilantro, chopped
- Juice of 1 lime
- Salt and pepper to taste

Instructions:

In a bowl, combine the diced avocados, diced tomato, finely chopped red onion, chopped jalapeño, and chopped cilantro.
Squeeze the juice of 1 lime over the mixture. Adjust the lime juice to your taste.
Gently toss the ingredients together until well combined, being careful not to mash the avocados too much.
Season the avocado salsa with salt and pepper to taste. Start with a small amount and adjust as needed.
Allow the salsa to sit in the refrigerator for at least 15-30 minutes before serving to let the flavors meld.
Before serving, give the avocado salsa a final stir and adjust the seasoning if necessary.
Serve this Avocado Salsa as a delicious topping for grilled chicken, fish, or shrimp. It's also perfect as a dip for tortilla chips or as a side for tacos.

Enjoy the creamy texture and vibrant flavors of this Avocado Salsa!

Tomatillo Salsa Verde

Ingredients:

- 1 pound tomatillos, husked and washed
- 1/2 white onion, coarsely chopped
- 2 cloves garlic, peeled
- 1-2 jalapeño peppers, stemmed and seeded (adjust for spice preference)
- 1/2 cup fresh cilantro, chopped
- Juice of 2 limes
- Salt to taste

Instructions:

Preheat your broiler.
Place the tomatillos on a baking sheet and broil for about 5-7 minutes, turning occasionally until they are lightly charred and softened.
In a blender or food processor, combine the broiled tomatillos, coarsely chopped onion, garlic, jalapeño peppers, cilantro, and lime juice.
Pulse the ingredients until you achieve a smooth consistency. If you prefer a chunkier salsa, pulse fewer times.
Taste the salsa and add salt to your liking. Pulse again to combine.
Allow the Tomatillo Salsa Verde to cool to room temperature, and then refrigerate for at least 30 minutes before serving to let the flavors meld.
Before serving, give the salsa a final stir.
Serve the Tomatillo Salsa Verde as a flavorful accompaniment to tacos, grilled meats, or as a dip for tortilla chips.

Enjoy the tangy and vibrant flavors of this Tomatillo Salsa Verde!

Cilantro Lime Salsa

Ingredients:

- 1 cup fresh tomatoes, diced
- 1/2 red onion, finely chopped
- 1/4 cup fresh cilantro, chopped
- 1 jalapeño pepper, seeded and finely chopped
- Juice of 2 limes
- 1 clove garlic, minced
- Salt and pepper to taste

Instructions:

In a bowl, combine the diced tomatoes, finely chopped red onion, chopped cilantro, chopped jalapeño, and minced garlic.
Squeeze the juice of 2 limes over the mixture.
Gently toss the ingredients together until well combined.
Season the Cilantro Lime Salsa with salt and pepper to taste. Start with a small amount and adjust as needed.
Allow the salsa to chill in the refrigerator for at least 15-30 minutes before serving to let the flavors meld.
Before serving, give the salsa a final stir and adjust the seasoning if necessary.
Serve this Cilantro Lime Salsa as a zesty topping for grilled chicken, fish, or tacos. It's also perfect with tortilla chips!

Enjoy the bright and citrusy flavors of this Cilantro Lime Salsa!

Chipotle Tomato Salsa

Ingredients:

- 4 medium tomatoes, diced
- 1/2 red onion, finely chopped
- 2 chipotle peppers in adobo sauce, finely chopped
- 2 cloves garlic, minced
- 1/4 cup fresh cilantro, chopped
- Juice of 1 lime
- 1 tablespoon adobo sauce (from the chipotle pepper can)
- Salt and pepper to taste

Instructions:

In a bowl, combine the diced tomatoes, finely chopped red onion, chopped chipotle peppers, minced garlic, and chopped cilantro.
In a separate small bowl, mix together the lime juice and adobo sauce.
Pour the lime and adobo mixture over the salsa ingredients.
Gently toss the ingredients together until well combined.
Season the Chipotle Tomato Salsa with salt and pepper to taste. Start with a small amount and adjust as needed.
Allow the salsa to chill in the refrigerator for at least 15-30 minutes before serving to let the flavors meld.
Before serving, give the salsa a final stir and adjust the seasoning if necessary.
Serve this Chipotle Tomato Salsa as a smoky and spicy topping for grilled meats, tacos, or as a dip for tortilla chips.

Enjoy the bold and smoky flavors of this Chipotle Tomato Salsa!

Watermelon Mint Salsa

Ingredients:

- 2 cups diced seedless watermelon
- 1/2 red onion, finely chopped
- 1/4 cup fresh mint leaves, finely chopped
- 1 jalapeño pepper, seeded and finely chopped
- Juice of 1 lime
- Salt to taste

Instructions:

In a bowl, combine the diced watermelon, finely chopped red onion, chopped mint leaves, and chopped jalapeño.

Squeeze the juice of 1 lime over the mixture.

Gently toss the ingredients together until well combined.

Season the Watermelon Mint Salsa with salt to taste. Start with a small amount and adjust as needed.

Allow the salsa to chill in the refrigerator for at least 15-30 minutes before serving to let the flavors meld.

Before serving, give the salsa a final stir and adjust the seasoning if necessary.

Serve this Watermelon Mint Salsa as a refreshing and sweet side for grilled chicken, fish, or as a unique topping for tacos. It's also great with tortilla chips!

Enjoy the cool and summery flavors of this Watermelon Mint Salsa!

Grilled Peach Salsa

Ingredients:

- 3 ripe peaches, halved and pitted
- 1/2 red onion, finely chopped
- 1 jalapeño pepper, seeded and finely chopped
- 1/4 cup fresh cilantro, chopped
- Juice of 1 lime
- 1 tablespoon olive oil
- Salt and pepper to taste

Instructions:

Preheat your grill or grill pan over medium-high heat.
Lightly brush the peach halves with olive oil.
Grill the peaches for about 2-3 minutes per side or until grill marks appear, and the peaches are softened.
Remove the grilled peaches from the heat and let them cool slightly. Once cooled, dice the peaches.
In a bowl, combine the diced grilled peaches, finely chopped red onion, chopped jalapeño, and chopped cilantro.
Squeeze the juice of 1 lime over the mixture.
Gently toss the ingredients together until well combined.
Season the Grilled Peach Salsa with salt and pepper to taste. Start with a small amount and adjust as needed.
Allow the salsa to chill in the refrigerator for at least 15-30 minutes before serving to let the flavors meld.
Before serving, give the salsa a final stir and adjust the seasoning if necessary.
Serve this Grilled Peach Salsa as a sweet and smoky topping for grilled chicken, pork, or as a unique side for tacos. It's also fantastic with tortilla chips!

Enjoy the delightful combination of grilled peaches and savory flavors in this salsa!

Roasted Red Pepper Salsa

Ingredients:

- 2 red bell peppers
- 1 can (14 oz) diced tomatoes, drained
- 1/2 red onion, finely chopped
- 2 cloves garlic, minced
- 1 jalapeño pepper, seeded and finely chopped
- 2 tablespoons olive oil
- Juice of 1 lime
- 1/4 cup fresh cilantro, chopped
- Salt and pepper to taste

Instructions:

Preheat your oven's broiler.
Place the red bell peppers on a baking sheet and broil for 10-15 minutes, turning occasionally, until the skins are charred and blistered.
Remove the peppers from the oven and place them in a bowl. Cover the bowl with plastic wrap and let the peppers steam for about 10 minutes. This will make it easier to peel off the skins.
Peel, seed, and dice the roasted red peppers.
In a bowl, combine the diced roasted red peppers, drained diced tomatoes, finely chopped red onion, minced garlic, chopped jalapeño, and chopped cilantro.
In a separate small bowl, whisk together the olive oil and lime juice.
Pour the olive oil and lime mixture over the salsa ingredients.
Gently toss everything together until well combined.
Season the Roasted Red Pepper Salsa with salt and pepper to taste. Start with a small amount and adjust as needed.
Allow the salsa to chill in the refrigerator for at least 15-30 minutes before serving to let the flavors meld.
Before serving, give the salsa a final stir and adjust the seasoning if necessary.
Serve this Roasted Red Pepper Salsa as a smoky and vibrant topping for grilled meats, fish, or as a dip for tortilla chips.

Enjoy the rich and roasted flavor of this delightful Red Pepper Salsa!

Three-Bean Dip

Ingredients:

- 1 can (15 oz) black beans, drained and rinsed
- 1 can (15 oz) kidney beans, drained and rinsed
- 1 can (15 oz) cannellini beans, drained and rinsed
- 1/2 cup corn kernels (fresh or frozen, thawed)
- 1/2 red onion, finely chopped
- 1 red bell pepper, diced
- 1 jalapeño pepper, seeded and finely chopped
- 2 cloves garlic, minced
- 1/4 cup fresh cilantro, chopped
- Juice of 2 limes
- 1 teaspoon ground cumin
- Salt and pepper to taste
- 1 cup shredded cheddar or Mexican blend cheese (optional)
- Tortilla chips for serving

Instructions:

In a large bowl, combine the black beans, kidney beans, cannellini beans, corn kernels, finely chopped red onion, diced red bell pepper, chopped jalapeño, minced garlic, and chopped cilantro.
In a separate small bowl, whisk together the lime juice and ground cumin.
Pour the lime and cumin mixture over the bean mixture.
Gently toss everything together until well combined.
Season the Three-Bean Dip with salt and pepper to taste. Start with a small amount and adjust as needed.
If using cheese, fold in the shredded cheddar or Mexican blend cheese.
Allow the dip to chill in the refrigerator for at least 30 minutes before serving to let the flavors meld.
Before serving, give the Three-Bean Dip a final stir and adjust the seasoning if necessary.
Serve the dip with tortilla chips or vegetable sticks.

Enjoy this hearty and flavorful Three-Bean Dip as a crowd-pleasing appetizer!

Guacamole

Ingredients:

- 3 ripe avocados
- 1/2 red onion, finely diced
- 1-2 tomatoes, diced
- 1 jalapeño pepper, seeded and finely chopped
- 2 cloves garlic, minced
- Juice of 1-2 limes
- 1/4 cup fresh cilantro, chopped
- Salt and pepper to taste

Instructions:

Cut the avocados in half, remove the pits, and scoop the flesh into a bowl.
Mash the avocados using a fork or potato masher, leaving some chunks for texture.
Add the finely diced red onion, diced tomatoes, chopped jalapeño, minced garlic, and chopped cilantro to the mashed avocados.
Squeeze the juice of 1-2 limes over the mixture. Adjust the lime juice to your taste.
Gently fold all the ingredients together until well combined.
Season the guacamole with salt and pepper to taste. Start with a small amount and adjust as needed.
Optionally, garnish with extra cilantro on top.
Allow the guacamole to chill in the refrigerator for at least 15-30 minutes before serving to let the flavors meld.
Before serving, give the guacamole a final stir and adjust the seasoning if necessary.
Serve the guacamole with tortilla chips, tacos, or as a topping for grilled meats.

Enjoy the creamy and flavorful goodness of homemade guacamole!

Queso Blanco Dip

Ingredients:

- 1 tablespoon butter
- 1 small onion, finely diced
- 2 cloves garlic, minced
- 2 tablespoons all-purpose flour
- 1 cup whole milk
- 8 oz white American cheese, shredded
- 4 oz Monterey Jack cheese, shredded
- 1 can (4 oz) diced green chilies, drained
- 1/2 teaspoon ground cumin
- Salt and pepper to taste
- Chopped fresh cilantro for garnish (optional)
- Sliced jalapeños for garnish (optional)
- Tortilla chips for serving

Instructions:

In a medium-sized saucepan, melt the butter over medium heat.
Add the finely diced onion and cook until softened, about 3-4 minutes.
Add the minced garlic and cook for an additional 1 minute until fragrant.
Sprinkle the flour over the onion and garlic, stirring constantly to create a roux. Cook for 1-2 minutes until the flour is lightly golden.
Gradually whisk in the whole milk, ensuring there are no lumps. Continue to cook and whisk until the mixture thickens.
Reduce the heat to low and gradually add the shredded white American cheese and Monterey Jack cheese, stirring continuously until the cheese is fully melted and smooth.
Stir in the diced green chilies and ground cumin. Season with salt and pepper to taste.
Once the dip is smooth and well combined, remove it from heat.
If desired, garnish with chopped fresh cilantro and sliced jalapeños.
Serve the Queso Blanco Dip warm with tortilla chips for dipping.

Enjoy this creamy and flavorful Queso Blanco Dip as a crowd-pleasing appetizer!

Spinach and Artichoke Dip

Ingredients:

- 1 (10 oz) package frozen chopped spinach, thawed and drained
- 1 (14 oz) can artichoke hearts, drained and chopped
- 1/2 cup mayonnaise
- 1/2 cup sour cream
- 1 cup shredded mozzarella cheese
- 1/2 cup grated Parmesan cheese
- 1 clove garlic, minced
- 1/2 teaspoon onion powder
- 1/2 teaspoon dried oregano
- 1/4 teaspoon black pepper
- Salt to taste
- Tortilla chips, sliced baguette, or vegetable sticks for serving

Instructions:

Preheat your oven to 375°F (190°C).
In a large bowl, combine the thawed and drained chopped spinach with the chopped artichoke hearts.
Add mayonnaise, sour cream, shredded mozzarella, grated Parmesan, minced garlic, onion powder, dried oregano, black pepper, and a pinch of salt.
Mix all the ingredients until well combined.
Transfer the mixture to a baking dish, spreading it evenly.
Bake in the preheated oven for 25-30 minutes or until the top is golden brown and the dip is bubbling.
Remove from the oven and let it cool for a few minutes before serving.
Serve the Spinach and Artichoke Dip with tortilla chips, sliced baguette, or vegetable sticks.

Enjoy this warm and creamy Spinach and Artichoke Dip as a crowd-pleasing appetizer!

Jalapeño Popper Dip

Ingredients:

- 8 oz cream cheese, softened
- 1/2 cup mayonnaise
- 1 cup shredded cheddar cheese
- 1 cup shredded Monterey Jack cheese
- 1/2 cup grated Parmesan cheese
- 1 cup diced pickled jalapeños, drained
- 1 cup breadcrumbs
- 1/2 cup cooked and crumbled bacon (optional)
- 1/4 cup chopped fresh chives (optional)
- Tortilla chips or sliced baguette for serving

Instructions:

Preheat your oven to 375°F (190°C).

In a large mixing bowl, combine the softened cream cheese and mayonnaise. Mix until smooth and well combined.

Add the shredded cheddar cheese, shredded Monterey Jack cheese, grated Parmesan cheese, and diced pickled jalapeños to the bowl. Mix until all ingredients are evenly distributed.

Transfer the mixture to a baking dish, spreading it evenly.

In a small bowl, combine the breadcrumbs and, if desired, the crumbled bacon and chopped chives.

Sprinkle the breadcrumb mixture evenly over the cream cheese mixture in the baking dish.

Bake in the preheated oven for 25-30 minutes or until the top is golden brown and the dip is bubbling.

Remove from the oven and let it cool for a few minutes before serving.

Serve the Jalapeño Popper Dip with tortilla chips or sliced baguette.

Enjoy the spicy, cheesy goodness of this Jalapeño Popper Dip at your next gathering!

Corn and Jalapeño Dip

Ingredients:

- 2 cups frozen corn kernels, thawed
- 1 can (4 oz) diced green chilies, drained
- 1 jalapeño pepper, seeded and finely chopped
- 1 cup shredded cheddar cheese
- 1/2 cup mayonnaise
- 1/2 cup sour cream
- 1/2 cup grated Parmesan cheese
- 1/4 cup chopped fresh cilantro
- 1 teaspoon ground cumin
- 1/2 teaspoon garlic powder
- Salt and pepper to taste
- Tortilla chips or crackers for serving

Instructions:

Preheat your oven to 375°F (190°C).
In a large bowl, combine the thawed corn kernels, drained diced green chilies, chopped jalapeño, shredded cheddar cheese, mayonnaise, sour cream, grated Parmesan cheese, chopped cilantro, ground cumin, and garlic powder.
Mix all the ingredients until well combined.
Season the mixture with salt and pepper to taste. Start with a small amount and adjust as needed.
Transfer the mixture to a baking dish, spreading it evenly.
Bake in the preheated oven for 25-30 minutes or until the top is golden brown and the dip is bubbly.
Remove from the oven and let it cool for a few minutes before serving.
Serve the Corn and Jalapeño Dip with tortilla chips or crackers.

Enjoy this flavorful and slightly spicy Corn and Jalapeño Dip as a delightful appetizer!

Mango Avocado Salsa

Ingredients:

- 1 ripe mango, peeled, pitted, and diced
- 1 ripe avocado, peeled, pitted, and diced
- 1/2 red onion, finely chopped
- 1 jalapeño pepper, seeded and finely chopped
- 1/4 cup fresh cilantro, chopped
- Juice of 2 limes
- Salt and pepper to taste

Instructions:

In a bowl, combine the diced mango, diced avocado, finely chopped red onion, chopped jalapeño, and chopped cilantro.
Squeeze the juice of 2 limes over the mixture.
Gently toss the ingredients together until well combined, being careful not to mash the avocado too much.
Season the Mango Avocado Salsa with salt and pepper to taste. Start with a small amount and adjust as needed.
Allow the salsa to chill in the refrigerator for at least 15-30 minutes before serving to let the flavors meld.
Before serving, give the salsa a final stir and adjust the seasoning if necessary.
Serve this Mango Avocado Salsa as a refreshing topping for grilled chicken, fish, or as a dip for tortilla chips.

Enjoy the sweet and creamy combination of mango and avocado in this vibrant salsa!

Roasted Garlic Salsa

Ingredients:

- 6 large tomatoes, halved
- 1 onion, peeled and quartered
- 1 head of garlic, top trimmed to expose cloves
- 2 jalapeño peppers, stemmed and seeded
- 2 tablespoons olive oil
- Salt and pepper to taste
- 1/4 cup fresh cilantro, chopped
- Juice of 1 lime

Instructions:

Preheat your oven to 400°F (200°C).

Place the halved tomatoes, quartered onion, whole head of garlic, and jalapeño peppers on a baking sheet.

Drizzle the vegetables with olive oil and season with salt and pepper. Toss to coat evenly.

Roast the vegetables in the preheated oven for about 30-40 minutes or until the tomatoes and peppers are charred and softened.

Remove the baking sheet from the oven and let the roasted vegetables cool for a few minutes.

Squeeze the roasted garlic cloves out of their skins and place them in a food processor or blender.

Add the roasted tomatoes, onion, and jalapeño peppers to the food processor or blender.

Add chopped cilantro and lime juice.

Pulse the mixture until you achieve your desired salsa consistency. If you prefer a chunkier salsa, pulse fewer times.

Taste the salsa and adjust the seasoning with additional salt, pepper, or lime juice as needed.

Allow the Roasted Garlic Salsa to cool to room temperature, and then refrigerate for at least 30 minutes before serving to allow the flavors to meld.

Serve the salsa with tortilla chips, tacos, grilled meats, or your favorite Mexican dishes.

Enjoy the rich and smoky flavor of this Roasted Garlic Salsa!

Roasted Corn Salsa

Ingredients:

- 2 cups corn kernels (fresh or frozen, thawed)
- 1 red onion, finely chopped
- 1 red bell pepper, diced
- 1 jalapeño pepper, seeded and finely chopped
- 1/4 cup fresh cilantro, chopped
- Juice of 2 limes
- 2 tablespoons olive oil
- Salt and pepper to taste

Instructions:

Preheat your oven to 400°F (200°C).
If using fresh corn, shuck the corn and remove the silk. Place the corn on a baking sheet.
Roast the corn in the preheated oven for about 15-20 minutes or until the corn is lightly browned and has a roasted aroma. If using frozen corn, you can still roast it for a shorter time.
In a large bowl, combine the roasted corn, finely chopped red onion, diced red bell pepper, chopped jalapeño, and chopped cilantro.
In a small bowl, whisk together the lime juice and olive oil.
Pour the lime and olive oil mixture over the salsa ingredients.
Gently toss everything together until well combined.
Season the Roasted Corn Salsa with salt and pepper to taste. Start with a small amount and adjust as needed.
Allow the salsa to chill in the refrigerator for at least 15-30 minutes before serving to let the flavors meld.
Before serving, give the salsa a final stir and adjust the seasoning if necessary.
Serve the Roasted Corn Salsa with tortilla chips, grilled meats, tacos, or as a refreshing side dish.

Enjoy the sweet and smoky flavors of this Roasted Corn Salsa!

Black Bean and Corn Dip

Ingredients:

- 1 can (15 oz) black beans, drained and rinsed
- 1 cup corn kernels (fresh or frozen, thawed)
- 1 red bell pepper, diced
- 1/2 red onion, finely chopped
- 1 jalapeño pepper, seeded and finely chopped
- 1/4 cup fresh cilantro, chopped
- Juice of 2 limes
- 2 tablespoons olive oil
- 1 teaspoon ground cumin
- Salt and pepper to taste
- 1 cup shredded cheddar or Mexican blend cheese (optional)
- Tortilla chips for serving

Instructions:

In a large bowl, combine the drained and rinsed black beans, corn kernels, diced red bell pepper, finely chopped red onion, chopped jalapeño, and chopped cilantro.

In a small bowl, whisk together the lime juice, olive oil, ground cumin, salt, and pepper.

Pour the dressing over the black bean and corn mixture.

Gently toss everything together until the dip is well combined and coated in the dressing.

If using cheese, fold in the shredded cheddar or Mexican blend cheese.

Taste the Black Bean and Corn Dip and adjust the seasoning if needed, adding more salt, pepper, or lime juice according to your preferences.

Allow the dip to chill in the refrigerator for at least 30 minutes before serving to let the flavors meld.

Before serving, give the dip a final stir.

Serve the Black Bean and Corn Dip with tortilla chips.

Enjoy this flavorful and hearty Black Bean and Corn Dip as a crowd-pleasing appetizer!

Tomatillo Avocado Salsa

Ingredients:

- 4 tomatillos, husked and rinsed
- 2 ripe avocados, peeled, pitted, and diced
- 1/2 red onion, finely chopped
- 1 jalapeño pepper, seeded and finely chopped
- 1/4 cup fresh cilantro, chopped
- Juice of 2 limes
- Salt and pepper to taste

Instructions:

    Preheat your broiler.
    Place the tomatillos on a baking sheet and broil for about 5-7 minutes, turning occasionally until they are slightly charred and softened.
    Remove the tomatillos from the oven and let them cool for a few minutes.
    Once cooled, roughly chop the tomatillos.
    In a bowl, combine the chopped tomatillos, diced avocados, finely chopped red onion, chopped jalapeño, and chopped cilantro.
    Squeeze the juice of 2 limes over the mixture.
    Gently toss the ingredients together until well combined.
    Season the Tomatillo Avocado Salsa with salt and pepper to taste. Start with a small amount and adjust as needed.
    Allow the salsa to chill in the refrigerator for at least 15-30 minutes before serving to let the flavors meld.
    Before serving, give the salsa a final stir and adjust the seasoning if necessary.
    Serve this Tomatillo Avocado Salsa as a zesty topping for grilled chicken, fish, or tacos. It's also perfect with tortilla chips!

Enjoy the tangy and creamy combination of tomatillos and avocados in this refreshing salsa!

Roasted Poblano Salsa

Ingredients:

- 3 poblano peppers
- 2 large tomatoes, halved
- 1 onion, peeled and quartered
- 3 cloves garlic, unpeeled
- 1 jalapeño pepper, seeded (optional, for additional heat)
- 1/4 cup fresh cilantro, chopped
- Juice of 2 limes
- Salt and pepper to taste

Instructions:

Preheat your broiler or grill.

Place the poblano peppers, halved tomatoes, quartered onion, unpeeled garlic cloves, and jalapeño (if using) on a baking sheet or grill grates.

Roast the vegetables under the broiler or on the grill, turning occasionally, until the skins are charred and blistered. This process usually takes about 10-15 minutes.

Remove the vegetables from the heat and place the poblano peppers in a sealed plastic bag or covered bowl to steam for about 10 minutes. This makes it easier to peel the skins.

Once the poblano peppers are cool enough to handle, peel off the charred skins, remove the seeds, and dice the flesh.

Peel the roasted garlic cloves.

In a blender or food processor, combine the roasted poblano peppers, tomatoes, onion, peeled garlic, jalapeño (if used), cilantro, and lime juice.

Pulse the mixture until you achieve your desired salsa consistency. If you prefer a chunkier salsa, pulse fewer times.

Season the Roasted Poblano Salsa with salt and pepper to taste. Start with a small amount and adjust as needed.

Allow the salsa to chill in the refrigerator for at least 15-30 minutes before serving to let the flavors meld.

Before serving, give the salsa a final stir and adjust the seasoning if necessary.

Serve the Roasted Poblano Salsa with tortilla chips, tacos, grilled meats, or as a flavorful dip.

Enjoy the smoky and mild heat of this Roasted Poblano Salsa!

Cucumber Salsa

Ingredients:

- 2 large cucumbers, diced
- 1/2 red onion, finely chopped
- 1 bell pepper (any color), diced
- 1 jalapeño pepper, seeded and finely chopped
- 1/4 cup fresh cilantro, chopped
- Juice of 2 limes
- 2 tablespoons olive oil
- Salt and pepper to taste

Instructions:

In a bowl, combine the diced cucumbers, finely chopped red onion, diced bell pepper, chopped jalapeño, and chopped cilantro.
In a small bowl, whisk together the lime juice and olive oil.
Pour the lime and olive oil mixture over the cucumber mixture.
Gently toss everything together until well combined.
Season the Cucumber Salsa with salt and pepper to taste. Start with a small amount and adjust as needed.
Allow the salsa to chill in the refrigerator for at least 15-30 minutes before serving to let the flavors meld.
Before serving, give the salsa a final stir and adjust the seasoning if necessary.
Serve this Cucumber Salsa as a light and refreshing topping for grilled chicken, fish, or as a dip for tortilla chips.

Enjoy the crisp and cool flavors of this Cucumber Salsa!

Mexican Street Corn Dip

Ingredients:

- 4 cups corn kernels (fresh, frozen, or canned and drained)
- 1/2 cup mayonnaise
- 1/2 cup sour cream
- 1 cup crumbled cotija cheese
- 1/2 cup chopped fresh cilantro
- 1 jalapeño, seeded and finely chopped
- 1 clove garlic, minced
- Juice of 1 lime
- 1 teaspoon chili powder
- Salt and pepper to taste
- Tortilla chips for serving

Instructions:

In a large bowl, combine the corn kernels, mayonnaise, sour cream, crumbled cotija cheese, chopped cilantro, chopped jalapeño, minced garlic, and lime juice. Mix the ingredients until well combined.

Season the dip with chili powder, salt, and pepper to taste. Adjust the seasonings as needed.

Allow the Mexican Street Corn Dip to chill in the refrigerator for at least 30 minutes before serving to let the flavors meld.

Before serving, give the dip a final stir.

Serve the dip with tortilla chips for a delicious appetizer or party snack.

Enjoy the irresistible flavors of Mexican street corn in this creamy and savory dip!

Pineapple Mango Guacamole

Ingredients:

- 3 ripe avocados, peeled, pitted, and mashed
- 1 cup diced pineapple
- 1 cup diced mango
- 1/2 red onion, finely chopped
- 1 jalapeño pepper, seeded and finely chopped
- 1/4 cup fresh cilantro, chopped
- Juice of 2 limes
- Salt and pepper to taste

Instructions:

In a large bowl, combine the mashed avocados, diced pineapple, diced mango, finely chopped red onion, chopped jalapeño, and chopped cilantro.
Squeeze the juice of 2 limes over the mixture.
Gently toss the ingredients together until well combined, being careful not to mash the avocados too much.
Season the Pineapple Mango Guacamole with salt and pepper to taste. Start with a small amount and adjust as needed.
Allow the guacamole to chill in the refrigerator for at least 15-30 minutes before serving to let the flavors meld.
Before serving, give the guacamole a final stir and adjust the seasoning if necessary.
Serve this tropical guacamole with tortilla chips, as a topping for grilled chicken or fish, or as a side for tacos.

Enjoy the sweet and tangy twist of pineapple and mango in this delightful guacamole!

Habanero Peach Salsa

Ingredients:

- 2 ripe peaches, peeled, pitted, and diced
- 1 habanero pepper, seeded and finely chopped
- 1/2 red onion, finely chopped
- 1/4 cup fresh cilantro, chopped
- Juice of 2 limes
- Salt and pepper to taste

Instructions:

In a bowl, combine the diced peaches, finely chopped habanero pepper, finely chopped red onion, and chopped cilantro.
Squeeze the juice of 2 limes over the mixture.
Gently toss the ingredients together until well combined.
Season the Habanero Peach Salsa with salt and pepper to taste. Start with a small amount and adjust as needed.
Allow the salsa to chill in the refrigerator for at least 15-30 minutes before serving to let the flavors meld.
Before serving, give the salsa a final stir and adjust the seasoning if necessary.
Serve this Habanero Peach Salsa as a bold and spicy topping for grilled meats, fish, or as a fiery dip for tortilla chips.

Enjoy the sweet and fiery combination of peaches and habanero in this unique salsa!

Fajita Queso Dip

Ingredients:

- 1 tablespoon vegetable oil
- 1 pound chicken breast, thinly sliced
- 1 bell pepper, thinly sliced
- 1 onion, thinly sliced
- 1 teaspoon ground cumin
- 1 teaspoon chili powder
- 1/2 teaspoon smoked paprika
- 1/2 teaspoon garlic powder
- Salt and pepper to taste
- 1 can (10 oz) diced tomatoes with green chilies, undrained
- 1 package (16 oz) Velveeta cheese, cubed
- 1 cup shredded cheddar cheese
- 1/2 cup sour cream
- Tortilla chips for serving

Instructions:

In a large skillet, heat the vegetable oil over medium-high heat.
Add the sliced chicken breast to the skillet and cook until browned and cooked through.
Add the thinly sliced bell pepper and onion to the skillet. Cook until the vegetables are softened.
Sprinkle the ground cumin, chili powder, smoked paprika, garlic powder, salt, and pepper over the chicken and vegetables. Stir to combine.
Pour the can of diced tomatoes with green chilies (undrained) into the skillet. Stir well.
Reduce the heat to low and add the cubed Velveeta cheese and shredded cheddar cheese. Stir continuously until the cheese is melted and the mixture is smooth.
Once the cheese is melted, stir in the sour cream until well combined.
Taste the queso dip and adjust the seasonings if necessary.
Serve the Fajita Queso Dip warm with tortilla chips for dipping.

Enjoy this savory and cheesy Fajita Queso Dip as a crowd-pleasing appetizer or party snack!

Creamy Jalapeño Dip

Ingredients:

- 1 cup mayonnaise
- 1 cup sour cream
- 1 cup fresh cilantro, chopped
- 3-4 fresh jalapeño peppers, seeds removed and chopped
- 3 cloves garlic, minced
- Juice of 2 limes
- 1 teaspoon ground cumin
- 1/2 teaspoon onion powder
- Salt and pepper to taste

Instructions:

In a blender or food processor, combine mayonnaise, sour cream, chopped cilantro, chopped jalapeños, minced garlic, lime juice, ground cumin, and onion powder.
Blend the ingredients until you achieve a smooth and creamy consistency.
Taste the dip and season with salt and pepper to your liking. Adjust the lime juice, jalapeños, or cilantro if needed.
Transfer the Creamy Jalapeño Dip to a serving bowl.
Chill the dip in the refrigerator for at least 30 minutes before serving. This allows the flavors to meld and enhances the overall taste.
Before serving, give the dip a final stir and adjust the seasoning if necessary.
Serve the dip with tortilla chips, fresh vegetables, or as a delicious accompaniment to grilled meats.

Enjoy the zesty and creamy kick of this flavorful Jalapeño Dip!

Green Olive and Jalapeño Salsa

Ingredients:

- 1 cup green olives, pitted and chopped
- 2 jalapeño peppers, seeds removed and finely chopped
- 1/2 red onion, finely chopped
- 2 cloves garlic, minced
- 1/4 cup fresh cilantro, chopped
- Juice of 2 limes
- 2 tablespoons olive oil
- Salt and pepper to taste

Instructions:

In a bowl, combine the chopped green olives, finely chopped jalapeños, finely chopped red onion, minced garlic, and chopped cilantro.
Squeeze the juice of 2 limes over the mixture.
Drizzle olive oil over the salsa ingredients.
Gently toss everything together until well combined.
Season the Green Olive and Jalapeño Salsa with salt and pepper to taste. Start with a small amount and adjust as needed.
Allow the salsa to chill in the refrigerator for at least 15-30 minutes before serving to let the flavors meld.
Before serving, give the salsa a final stir and adjust the seasoning if necessary.
Serve this Green Olive and Jalapeño Salsa with tortilla chips, grilled meats, or as a unique topping for tacos.

Enjoy the bold and briny flavor combination of green olives and jalapeños in this distinctive salsa!

Charred Tomato and Onion Salsa

Ingredients:

- 4 large tomatoes, halved
- 1 large onion, peeled and quartered
- 2 cloves garlic, unpeeled
- 1 jalapeño pepper, stemmed and seeded
- 1/4 cup fresh cilantro, chopped
- Juice of 2 limes
- Salt and pepper to taste

Instructions:

Preheat your broiler or grill.
Place the tomato halves, quartered onion, unpeeled garlic cloves, and jalapeño pepper on a baking sheet or grill grates.
Char the vegetables under the broiler or on the grill, turning occasionally, until the skins are charred and the vegetables are softened. This usually takes about 10-15 minutes.
Remove the vegetables from the heat and let them cool for a few minutes.
Once cooled, peel the skin off the garlic cloves and discard.
In a food processor or blender, combine the charred tomatoes, onions, garlic, jalapeño, and cilantro.
Pulse the mixture until you achieve your desired salsa consistency. If you prefer a chunkier salsa, pulse fewer times.
Transfer the salsa to a bowl.
Squeeze the juice of 2 limes over the salsa and stir to combine.
Season the Charred Tomato and Onion Salsa with salt and pepper to taste. Start with a small amount and adjust as needed.
Allow the salsa to chill in the refrigerator for at least 15-30 minutes before serving to let the flavors meld.
Before serving, give the salsa a final stir and adjust the seasoning if necessary.
Serve the Charred Tomato and Onion Salsa with tortilla chips, tacos, or grilled meats.

Enjoy the smoky and savory goodness of this Charred Tomato and Onion Salsa!

Tequila Lime Salsa

Ingredients:

- 4 large tomatoes, diced
- 1 red onion, finely chopped
- 1 jalapeño pepper, seeded and finely chopped
- 1/4 cup fresh cilantro, chopped
- Juice of 2 limes
- 2 tablespoons tequila
- 1 tablespoon orange juice
- Salt and pepper to taste

Instructions:

In a bowl, combine the diced tomatoes, finely chopped red onion, chopped jalapeño, and chopped cilantro.
In a small bowl, whisk together the lime juice, tequila, and orange juice.
Pour the tequila-lime mixture over the salsa ingredients.
Gently toss everything together until well combined.
Season the Tequila Lime Salsa with salt and pepper to taste. Start with a small amount and adjust as needed.
Allow the salsa to chill in the refrigerator for at least 15-30 minutes before serving to let the flavors meld.
Before serving, give the salsa a final stir and adjust the seasoning if necessary.
Serve this Tequila Lime Salsa with tortilla chips, grilled chicken, fish, or as a refreshing topping for tacos.

Enjoy the vibrant and citrusy kick of this Tequila Lime Salsa!

Smoky Chipotle Guacamole

Ingredients:

- 3 ripe avocados
- 1/2 red onion, finely diced
- 1-2 tomatoes, diced
- 1-2 chipotle peppers in adobo sauce, finely chopped
- 2 cloves garlic, minced
- Juice of 1-2 limes
- 1/4 cup fresh cilantro, chopped
- Salt and pepper to taste

Instructions:

Cut the avocados in half, remove the pits, and scoop the flesh into a bowl.
Mash the avocados using a fork or potato masher, leaving some chunks for texture.
Add the finely diced red onion, diced tomatoes, chopped chipotle peppers, minced garlic, and chopped cilantro to the mashed avocados.
Squeeze the juice of 1-2 limes over the mixture. Adjust the lime juice to your taste.
Gently fold all the ingredients together until well combined.
Season the Smoky Chipotle Guacamole with salt and pepper to taste. Start with a small amount and adjust as needed.
Allow the guacamole to chill in the refrigerator for at least 15-30 minutes before serving to let the flavors meld.
Before serving, give the guacamole a final stir and adjust the seasoning if necessary.
Serve the Smoky Chipotle Guacamole with tortilla chips, tacos, or as a topping for grilled meats.

Enjoy the bold and smoky flavor of chipotle in this delicious guacamole!

Avocado Lime Crema

Ingredients:

- 1 ripe avocado
- 1/2 cup sour cream

- Juice of 1 lime
- 2 tablespoons fresh cilantro, chopped
- Salt and pepper to taste

Instructions:

Cut the avocado in half, remove the pit, and scoop the flesh into a blender or food processor.
Add sour cream, lime juice, and chopped cilantro to the blender or food processor.
Blend until the mixture is smooth and creamy.
Season the Avocado Lime Crema with salt and pepper to taste. Start with a small amount and adjust as needed.
Transfer the crema to a bowl.
Refrigerate the Avocado Lime Crema for at least 15-30 minutes before serving to allow the flavors to meld.
Before serving, give the crema a final stir and adjust the seasoning if necessary.
Serve the Avocado Lime Crema as a topping for tacos, grilled meats, or as a dip for tortilla chips.

Enjoy the creamy and zesty goodness of this Avocado Lime Crema!

Creamy Black Bean Dip

Ingredients:

- 1 can (15 oz) black beans, drained and rinsed
- 1/2 cup sour cream
- 1/4 cup mayonnaise
- 1 cup shredded cheddar cheese
- 1 clove garlic, minced
- 1 teaspoon ground cumin
- 1/2 teaspoon chili powder
- 1/4 teaspoon cayenne pepper (optional, for heat)
- Juice of 1 lime
- Salt and pepper to taste
- Fresh cilantro for garnish (optional)
- Tortilla chips for serving

Instructions:

In a food processor or blender, combine the black beans, sour cream, mayonnaise, shredded cheddar cheese, minced garlic, ground cumin, chili powder, cayenne pepper (if using), and lime juice.
Blend the ingredients until you achieve a smooth and creamy consistency.
Season the Creamy Black Bean Dip with salt and pepper to taste. Start with a small amount and adjust as needed.
Transfer the dip to a serving bowl.
If desired, garnish with fresh cilantro.
Refrigerate the dip for at least 30 minutes before serving to allow the flavors to meld.
Before serving, give the dip a final stir and adjust the seasoning if necessary.
Serve the Creamy Black Bean Dip with tortilla chips for dipping.

Enjoy this delicious and creamy dip as a snack or appetizer!

Roasted Hatch Chile Salsa

Ingredients:

- 4-6 Hatch chile peppers
- 4 large tomatoes, halved
- 1 onion, peeled and quartered
- 3 cloves garlic, unpeeled
- 1/4 cup fresh cilantro, chopped
- Juice of 2 limes
- Salt and pepper to taste

Instructions:

Preheat your broiler or grill.
Place the Hatch chile peppers, halved tomatoes, quartered onion, and unpeeled garlic cloves on a baking sheet or grill grates.
Roast the vegetables under the broiler or on the grill, turning occasionally, until the skins are charred and the vegetables are softened. This usually takes about 10-15 minutes.
Remove the vegetables from the heat and let them cool for a few minutes.
Once cooled, peel the skin off the garlic cloves.
In a blender or food processor, combine the roasted Hatch chile peppers, tomatoes, onion, peeled garlic, and cilantro.
Pulse the mixture until you achieve your desired salsa consistency. If you prefer a chunkier salsa, pulse fewer times.
Transfer the salsa to a bowl.
Squeeze the juice of 2 limes over the salsa and stir to combine.
Season the Roasted Hatch Chile Salsa with salt and pepper to taste. Start with a small amount and adjust as needed.
Allow the salsa to chill in the refrigerator for at least 15-30 minutes before serving to let the flavors meld.
Before serving, give the salsa a final stir and adjust the seasoning if necessary.
Serve the Roasted Hatch Chile Salsa with tortilla chips, tacos, or grilled meats.

Enjoy the smoky and spicy flavor of this Roasted Hatch Chile Salsa!

Roasted Serrano Salsa

Ingredients:

- 6-8 serrano peppers
- 4 large tomatoes, halved
- 1 onion, peeled and quartered
- 3 cloves garlic, unpeeled
- 1/4 cup fresh cilantro, chopped
- Juice of 2 limes
- Salt and pepper to taste

Instructions:

Preheat your broiler or grill.
Place the serrano peppers, halved tomatoes, quartered onion, and unpeeled garlic cloves on a baking sheet or grill grates.
Roast the vegetables under the broiler or on the grill, turning occasionally, until the skins are charred and the vegetables are softened. This usually takes about 10-15 minutes.
Remove the vegetables from the heat and let them cool for a few minutes.
Once cooled, peel the skin off the garlic cloves.
In a blender or food processor, combine the roasted serrano peppers, tomatoes, onion, peeled garlic, and cilantro.
Pulse the mixture until you achieve your desired salsa consistency. If you prefer a chunkier salsa, pulse fewer times.
Transfer the salsa to a bowl.
Squeeze the juice of 2 limes over the salsa and stir to combine.
Season the Roasted Serrano Salsa with salt and pepper to taste. Start with a small amount and adjust as needed.
Allow the salsa to chill in the refrigerator for at least 15-30 minutes before serving to let the flavors meld.
Before serving, give the salsa a final stir and adjust the seasoning if necessary.
Serve the Roasted Serrano Salsa with tortilla chips, tacos, or grilled meats.

Enjoy the bold and fiery flavor of this Roasted Serrano Salsa!

Roasted Pineapple Habanero Salsa

Ingredients:

- 2 cups diced pineapple
- 2 habanero peppers, seeds removed and finely chopped
- 1 red onion, finely chopped
- 1/4 cup fresh cilantro, chopped
- Juice of 2 limes
- 2 tablespoons olive oil
- Salt and pepper to taste

Instructions:

Preheat your oven to 400°F (200°C).
Place the diced pineapple on a baking sheet.
Roast the pineapple in the preheated oven for about 15-20 minutes or until it's golden brown and caramelized. Keep an eye on it to prevent burning.
In a bowl, combine the roasted pineapple, finely chopped habanero peppers, finely chopped red onion, and chopped cilantro.
In a small bowl, whisk together the lime juice and olive oil.
Pour the lime and olive oil mixture over the salsa ingredients.
Gently toss everything together until well combined.
Season the Roasted Pineapple Habanero Salsa with salt and pepper to taste. Start with a small amount and adjust as needed.
Allow the salsa to chill in the refrigerator for at least 15-30 minutes before serving to let the flavors meld.
Before serving, give the salsa a final stir and adjust the seasoning if necessary.
Serve this sweet and spicy salsa with tortilla chips, grilled chicken, fish, or as a topping for tacos.

Enjoy the tropical and fiery kick of this Roasted Pineapple Habanero Salsa!

Mango Habanero Guacamole

Ingredients:

- 3 ripe avocados
- 1 ripe mango, peeled, pitted, and diced
- 1-2 habanero peppers, seeds removed and finely chopped
- 1/2 red onion, finely chopped
- 1/4 cup fresh cilantro, chopped
- Juice of 2 limes
- Salt and pepper to taste

Instructions:

Cut the avocados in half, remove the pits, and scoop the flesh into a bowl.
Mash the avocados using a fork or potato masher, leaving some chunks for texture.
Add the diced mango, finely chopped habanero peppers, finely chopped red onion, chopped cilantro, and lime juice to the mashed avocados.
Gently fold all the ingredients together until well combined.
Season the Mango Habanero Guacamole with salt and pepper to taste. Start with a small amount and adjust as needed.
Allow the guacamole to chill in the refrigerator for at least 15-30 minutes before serving to let the flavors meld.
Before serving, give the guacamole a final stir and adjust the seasoning if necessary.
Serve the Mango Habanero Guacamole with tortilla chips, tacos, or as a topping for grilled meats.

Enjoy the sweet and spicy fusion of mango and habanero in this tropical guacamole!

Mango Habanero Guacamole

Ingredients:

- 3 ripe avocados
- 1 ripe mango, peeled, pitted, and diced
- 1-2 habanero peppers, seeds removed and finely chopped
- 1/2 red onion, finely chopped
- 1/4 cup fresh cilantro, chopped
- Juice of 2 limes
- Salt and pepper to taste

Instructions:

Cut the avocados in half, remove the pits, and scoop the flesh into a bowl.
Mash the avocados using a fork or potato masher, leaving some chunks for texture.
Add the diced mango, finely chopped habanero peppers, finely chopped red onion, chopped cilantro, and lime juice to the mashed avocados.
Gently fold all the ingredients together until well combined.
Season the Mango Habanero Guacamole with salt and pepper to taste. Start with a small amount and adjust as needed.
Allow the guacamole to chill in the refrigerator for at least 15-30 minutes before serving to let the flavors meld.
Before serving, give the guacamole a final stir and adjust the seasoning if necessary.
Serve the Mango Habanero Guacamole with tortilla chips, tacos, or as a topping for grilled meats.

Enjoy the sweet and spicy fusion of mango and habanero in this tropical guacamole!

Cilantro Lime Crema

Ingredients:

- 1 cup sour cream
- 1/4 cup fresh cilantro, chopped
- Juice of 1 lime
- 1 clove garlic, minced
- Salt and pepper to taste

Instructions:

In a bowl, combine the sour cream, chopped cilantro, minced garlic, and lime juice.
Whisk the ingredients together until well combined.
Season the Cilantro Lime Crema with salt and pepper to taste. Start with a small amount and adjust as needed.
Allow the crema to chill in the refrigerator for at least 30 minutes before serving. This allows the flavors to meld and enhances the overall taste.
Before serving, give the crema a final stir.
Serve the Cilantro Lime Crema as a topping for tacos, grilled meats, or as a dip for tortilla chips.

Enjoy the fresh and zesty flavor of this Cilantro Lime Crema!

Black-Eyed Pea Salsa

Ingredients:

- 2 cans (15 oz each) black-eyed peas, drained and rinsed
- 1 cup corn kernels (fresh, frozen, or canned and drained)
- 1 red bell pepper, finely chopped
- 1/2 red onion, finely chopped
- 1 jalapeño pepper, seeded and finely chopped
- 1/4 cup fresh cilantro, chopped
- Juice of 2 limes
- 2 tablespoons olive oil
- 1 teaspoon ground cumin
- Salt and pepper to taste
- Tortilla chips for serving

Instructions:

In a large bowl, combine the black-eyed peas, corn kernels, finely chopped red bell pepper, finely chopped red onion, chopped jalapeño, and chopped cilantro.
In a small bowl, whisk together the lime juice, olive oil, ground cumin, salt, and pepper.
Pour the lime and olive oil mixture over the salsa ingredients.
Gently toss everything together until well combined.
Season the Black-Eyed Pea Salsa with additional salt and pepper to taste. Start with a small amount and adjust as needed.
Allow the salsa to chill in the refrigerator for at least 15-30 minutes before serving to let the flavors meld.
Before serving, give the salsa a final stir and adjust the seasoning if necessary.
Serve the Black-Eyed Pea Salsa with tortilla chips for a tasty appetizer or party snack.

Enjoy the hearty and flavorful combination of black-eyed peas, corn, and fresh veggies in this delicious salsa!

Chipotle Mango Salsa

Ingredients:

- 2 ripe mangoes, peeled, pitted, and diced
- 1 red bell pepper, finely chopped
- 1/2 red onion, finely chopped
- 1-2 chipotle peppers in adobo sauce, finely chopped
- 1/4 cup fresh cilantro, chopped
- Juice of 2 limes
- 1 tablespoon olive oil
- Salt and pepper to taste

Instructions:

In a bowl, combine the diced mangoes, finely chopped red bell pepper, finely chopped red onion, chopped chipotle peppers, and chopped cilantro.
In a small bowl, whisk together the lime juice and olive oil.
Pour the lime and olive oil mixture over the salsa ingredients.
Gently toss everything together until well combined.
Season the Chipotle Mango Salsa with salt and pepper to taste. Start with a small amount and adjust as needed.
Allow the salsa to chill in the refrigerator for at least 15-30 minutes before serving to let the flavors meld.
Before serving, give the salsa a final stir and adjust the seasoning if necessary.
Serve this Chipotle Mango Salsa with tortilla chips, grilled chicken, fish, or as a topping for tacos.

Enjoy the sweet and smoky flavors of mango and chipotle in this delicious salsa!

Tomatillo Guacamole

Ingredients:

- 3 ripe avocados
- 3 tomatillos, husked and finely chopped
- 1/2 red onion, finely chopped
- 1 jalapeño pepper, seeded and finely chopped
- 1/4 cup fresh cilantro, chopped
- Juice of 2 limes
- Salt and pepper to taste

Instructions:

Cut the avocados in half, remove the pits, and scoop the flesh into a bowl.
Mash the avocados using a fork or potato masher, leaving some chunks for texture.
Add the finely chopped tomatillos, finely chopped red onion, chopped jalapeño, chopped cilantro, and lime juice to the mashed avocados.
Gently fold all the ingredients together until well combined.
Season the Tomatillo Guacamole with salt and pepper to taste. Start with a small amount and adjust as needed.
Allow the guacamole to chill in the refrigerator for at least 15-30 minutes before serving to let the flavors meld.
Before serving, give the guacamole a final stir and adjust the seasoning if necessary.
Serve the Tomatillo Guacamole with tortilla chips, tacos, or as a topping for grilled meats.

Enjoy the fresh and tangy twist of tomatillos in this delicious guacamole!

Spicy Mango Pineapple Salsa

Ingredients:

- 1 ripe mango, peeled, pitted, and diced
- 1 cup fresh pineapple, diced
- 1 jalapeño pepper, seeded and finely chopped
- 1/2 red onion, finely chopped
- 1/4 cup fresh cilantro, chopped
- Juice of 2 limes
- 1 tablespoon honey or agave syrup (optional, for sweetness)
- Salt and pepper to taste

Instructions:

In a bowl, combine the diced mango, diced pineapple, finely chopped jalapeño, finely chopped red onion, and chopped cilantro.

Squeeze the juice of 2 limes over the mixture.

If you desire a touch of sweetness, add honey or agave syrup to the salsa. Adjust the sweetness to your liking.

Gently toss everything together until well combined.

Season the Spicy Mango Pineapple Salsa with salt and pepper to taste. Start with a small amount and adjust as needed.

Allow the salsa to chill in the refrigerator for at least 15-30 minutes before serving to let the flavors meld.

Before serving, give the salsa a final stir and adjust the seasoning if necessary.

Serve this Spicy Mango Pineapple Salsa with tortilla chips, grilled chicken or fish, or as a topping for tacos.

Enjoy the vibrant and tropical flavors of this spicy salsa!

Creamy Avocado Lime Salsa

Ingredients:

- 2 ripe avocados
- 1 small red onion, finely chopped
- 1 jalapeño, seeded and finely chopped
- 1/4 cup fresh cilantro, chopped
- Juice of 2 limes
- 1/4 cup sour cream
- Salt and pepper to taste

Instructions:

Cut the avocados in half, remove the pits, and scoop the flesh into a bowl.
Mash the avocados using a fork or potato masher, leaving some chunks for texture.
Add the finely chopped red onion, finely chopped jalapeño, chopped cilantro, lime juice, and sour cream to the mashed avocados.
Gently fold all the ingredients together until well combined.
Season the Creamy Avocado Lime Salsa with salt and pepper to taste. Start with a small amount and adjust as needed.
Allow the salsa to chill in the refrigerator for at least 15-30 minutes before serving to let the flavors meld.
Before serving, give the salsa a final stir and adjust the seasoning if necessary.
Serve the Creamy Avocado Lime Salsa with tortilla chips, tacos, or as a topping for grilled meats.

Enjoy the creamy and zesty goodness of this avocado lime salsa!

Roasted Garlic Guacamole

Ingredients:

- 3 ripe avocados
- 1 head of garlic
- 1 tablespoon olive oil
- 1 small red onion, finely chopped
- 1 jalapeño, seeded and finely chopped
- 1/4 cup fresh cilantro, chopped
- Juice of 2 limes
- Salt and pepper to taste

Instructions:

Preheat your oven to 400°F (200°C).
Cut the top off the head of garlic to expose the cloves, leaving the cloves attached to the base.
Place the garlic head on a piece of foil, drizzle it with olive oil, and wrap it in the foil.
Roast the garlic in the preheated oven for about 30-40 minutes or until the cloves are soft and golden.
Allow the roasted garlic to cool, then squeeze the roasted cloves out of their skins and mash them with a fork.
Cut the avocados in half, remove the pits, and scoop the flesh into a bowl.
Mash the avocados using a fork or potato masher, leaving some chunks for texture.
Add the mashed roasted garlic, finely chopped red onion, finely chopped jalapeño, chopped cilantro, and lime juice to the mashed avocados.
Gently fold all the ingredients together until well combined.
Season the Roasted Garlic Guacamole with salt and pepper to taste. Start with a small amount and adjust as needed.
Allow the guacamole to chill in the refrigerator for at least 15-30 minutes before serving to let the flavors meld.
Before serving, give the guacamole a final stir and adjust the seasoning if necessary.
Serve the Roasted Garlic Guacamole with tortilla chips, tacos, or as a topping for grilled meats.

Enjoy the rich and savory flavor of roasted garlic in this delicious guacamole!

Black Bean and Mango Salsa

Ingredients:

- 1 can (15 oz) black beans, drained and rinsed
- 1 ripe mango, peeled, pitted, and diced
- 1/2 red onion, finely chopped
- 1 red bell pepper, finely chopped
- 1 jalapeño, seeded and finely chopped
- 1/4 cup fresh cilantro, chopped
- Juice of 2 limes
- 2 tablespoons olive oil
- Salt and pepper to taste

Instructions:

In a large bowl, combine the black beans, diced mango, finely chopped red onion, finely chopped red bell pepper, chopped jalapeño, and chopped cilantro.
In a small bowl, whisk together the lime juice and olive oil.
Pour the lime and olive oil mixture over the salsa ingredients.
Gently toss everything together until well combined.
Season the Black Bean and Mango Salsa with salt and pepper to taste. Start with a small amount and adjust as needed.
Allow the salsa to chill in the refrigerator for at least 15-30 minutes before serving to let the flavors meld.
Before serving, give the salsa a final stir and adjust the seasoning if necessary.
Serve the Black Bean and Mango Salsa with tortilla chips, grilled chicken or fish, or as a topping for tacos.

Enjoy the sweet and savory combination of black beans and mango in this refreshing salsa!

Smoky Tomatillo Salsa

Ingredients:

- 6 tomatillos, husked and rinsed
- 2 poblano peppers
- 1 red onion, quartered
- 3 cloves garlic, unpeeled
- 1/4 cup fresh cilantro, chopped
- Juice of 2 limes
- 1 teaspoon ground cumin
- Salt and pepper to taste

Instructions:

Preheat your broiler or grill.

Place the tomatillos, poblano peppers, quartered red onion, and unpeeled garlic cloves on a baking sheet or grill grates.

Broil or grill the vegetables, turning occasionally, until the skins are charred and the vegetables are softened. This usually takes about 10-15 minutes.

Remove the vegetables from the heat and let them cool for a few minutes.

Once cooled, peel the skin off the garlic cloves.

In a blender or food processor, combine the roasted tomatillos, peeled poblano peppers, red onion, peeled garlic, chopped cilantro, lime juice, ground cumin, salt, and pepper.

Pulse the mixture until you achieve your desired salsa consistency. If you prefer a chunkier salsa, pulse fewer times.

Transfer the salsa to a bowl.

Allow the Smoky Tomatillo Salsa to chill in the refrigerator for at least 15-30 minutes before serving to let the flavors meld.

Before serving, give the salsa a final stir and adjust the seasoning if necessary.

Serve the Smoky Tomatillo Salsa with tortilla chips, tacos, or grilled meats.

Enjoy the smoky and tangy flavor of this delicious tomatillo salsa!

Roasted Jalapeño Guacamole

Ingredients:

- 3 ripe avocados
- 2-3 jalapeño peppers
- 1/2 red onion, finely chopped
- 1/4 cup fresh cilantro, chopped
- Juice of 2 limes
- 2 cloves garlic, minced
- Salt and pepper to taste

Instructions:

Preheat your oven broiler or grill.
Place the jalapeño peppers on a baking sheet or directly on the grill grates.
Roast the jalapeños under the broiler or on the grill, turning occasionally, until the skins are charred and blistered. This usually takes about 5-7 minutes.
Remove the jalapeños from the heat and let them cool for a few minutes.
Once cooled, peel the charred skin off the jalapeños, remove the seeds (if you prefer less heat), and finely chop them.
Cut the avocados in half, remove the pits, and scoop the flesh into a bowl.
Mash the avocados using a fork or potato masher, leaving some chunks for texture.
Add the finely chopped roasted jalapeños, finely chopped red onion, chopped cilantro, lime juice, and minced garlic to the mashed avocados.
Gently fold all the ingredients together until well combined.
Season the Roasted Jalapeño Guacamole with salt and pepper to taste. Start with a small amount and adjust as needed.
Allow the guacamole to chill in the refrigerator for at least 15-30 minutes before serving to let the flavors meld.
Before serving, give the guacamole a final stir and adjust the seasoning if necessary.
Serve the Roasted Jalapeño Guacamole with tortilla chips, tacos, or as a topping for grilled meats.

Enjoy the smoky and spicy kick of this Roasted Jalapeño Guacamole!

www.ingramcontent.com/pod-product-compliance
Lightning Source LLC
LaVergne TN
LVHW081322060526
838201LV00055B/2403